IRAN

David Downing

mc **Marshall Cavendish**
Benchmark
New York

This edition first published in 2009 in the United States of America by Marshall Cavendish Benchmark.

Marshall Cavendish Benchmark
99 White Plains Road
Tarrytown, NY 10591
www.marshallcavendish.us

All Internet sites were available and accurate when sent to press.

First published in 2008 by
MACMILLAN EDUCATION AUSTRALIA PTY LTD
15–19 Claremont Street, South Yarra 3141

Visit our website at www.macmillan.com.au or go directly to www.macmillanlibrary.com.au

Associated companies and representatives throughout the world.

National Library of Australia
Cataloguing-in-Publication data

Downing, David, 1946-
    Iran / by David Downing.
    p. cm. –(Global hotspots)
    Includes index.
    ISBN 978-0-7614-3179-4
    1.Iran–History–Juvenile literature.I. Title.
    DS254.75.D69 2008
    955–dc22

2008018692

 Produced for Macmillan Education Australia by
MONKEY PUZZLE MEDIA LTD
The Rectory, Eyke, Woodbridge, Suffolk IP12 2QW, UK

Edited by Susie Brooks
Text and cover design by Tom Morris and James Winrow
Page layout by Tom Morris
Photo research by Lynda Lines
Maps by Martin Darlison, Encompass Graphics

Printed in the United States

Acknowledgments
The author and the publisher are grateful to the following for permission to reproduce copyright material:

Front cover photograph: Iranian demostrators hold posters of Hezbollah chief Hassan Nasrallah during an anti-Israel protest in Tehran, 2006. Courtesy of Getty Images (AFP).

Corbis, pp. **6** (Bettman), **11** (Bettmann), **14** (Bettmann), **15** (Bettmann), **16** (Patrick Chauvel/Sygma), **18** (Bettmann), **19** (Christine Spengler/Sygma), **20** (Patrick Durand/Sygma), **21** (Jean Guichard/Sygma), **24** (Régis Bossu/Sygma), **25** (David Turnley), **29** (Kaveh Kazemi); Getty Images, pp. **4** (AFP), **8** (Mark Daffey), **10** (Hulton Archive), **12** (Hulton Archive), **13** (Time & Life Pictures), **17** (AFP), **22** (National Geographic), **23** (AFP), **26** (AFP), **28** (iStockphoto, p. **30**; Wikimedia Commons, p. **9**.

While every care has been taken to trace and acknowledge copyright, the publisher tenders their apologies for any accidental infringement where copyright has proved untraceable. Where the attempt has been unsuccessful, the publisher welcomes information that would redress the situation.

CONTENTS

Glossary words

When a word is printed in **bold**, you can look
up its meaning in the Glossary on page 31.

ALWAYS IN THE NEWS

Global hot spots are places that are always in the news. They are places where there has been conflict between different groups of people for years. Sometimes the conflicts have lasted for hundreds of years.

Why Do Hot Spots Happen?

There are four main reasons why hot spots happen:

1 Disputes over land, and who has the right to live on it.

2 Disagreements over religion and **culture**, where different peoples find it impossible to live happily side-by-side.

3 Arguments over how the government should be organized.

4 Conflict over resources, such as oil, gold, or diamonds.

Sometimes these disagreements spill over into violence—and into the headlines.

HOT SPOT BRIEFING

THE MIDDLE EAST
Iran is in the Middle East, along with Egypt, Israel, Palestine, Lebanon, Jordan, Syria, Iraq, and the countries of the **Arabian Peninsula**. Some definitions of the Middle East also include Turkey, Afghanistan, and the rest of North Africa.

Iranians wave their national flag during anniversary celebrations of the Islamic revolution, a major conflict over how the country should be governed.

Iran

Iran has been a hot spot since oil was found there in the early 1900s. Countries that use a lot of oil, such as Britain and the United States, began to get involved in Iranian affairs. Their involvement created conflict inside Iran, between supporters of a modern **Western** society and supporters of a more traditional, **Islamic** way of life.

A Revolution

In 1979, there was revolution in Iran. The **secular** ruler was overthrown by Islamic **traditionalists**, who took power. This upset a lot of people. Leaders of other Middle Eastern countries feared that they too would be thrown from power. The countries that relied on Iran's oil worried that the revolution might stop them having access to the oil they needed. Many people are still worried about these things today.

Iran lies between two seas, the Caspian Sea to the north and the Persian Gulf to the south. It has land borders with seven other countries. Tehran is the capital of Iran.

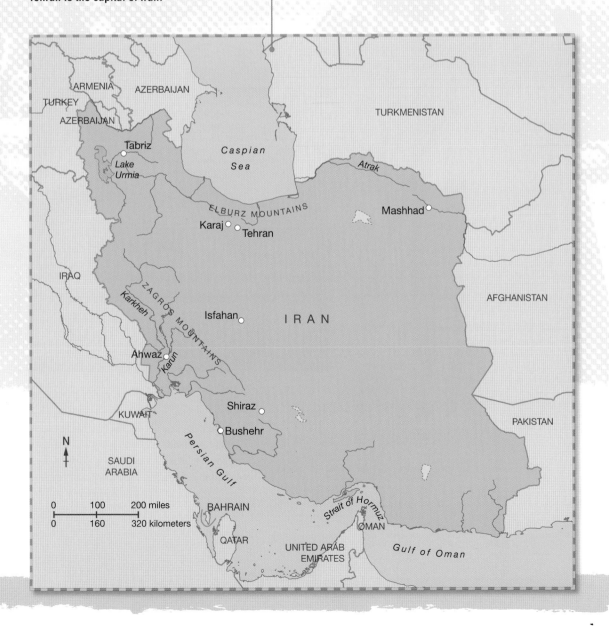

ANCIENT PERSIA

Until 1935, Iran was called Persia. The original Persians were **nomads** who came from Central Asia. Around 2000 BCE, they began settling in the upland areas of the country that is now Iran. From there, their **empire** grew as they moved to conquer new land.

The Persian Empire

By 530 BCE, the Persian Empire stretched from India to the Mediterranean Sea. It lasted for around 1,000 years. During this period, the Persians fought many wars against their powerful European neighbors–the Greeks first, and then the Romans.

HOT SPOT BRIEFING

THE LARGEST EMPIRE
The Emperor Cyrus the Great ruled Persia between 550 BCE and 530 BCE. The empire he created was, at the time, the largest the world had ever known.

This carving shows the Persian Emperor Darius I (549–485 BCE) with his son, the future emperor Xerxes I, behind him. Xerxes, who ruled from 485–465 BCE, led a great expedition against Greece which ended in failure.

A New Enemy

The Persian Empire was eventually destroyed by a new enemy, the Arabs. In the 600s, the Arabs wanted other nations to take on their new religion, Islam. They poured out of Arabia and conquered the whole of the Middle East and North Africa. Persia became a part of the new Arab Empire.

HOT SPOT BRIEFING

ISLAM

Islam was founded in Arabia by the Prophet Mohammed. After Mohammed's death in 632 CE, his followers spread the religion to other nations. Followers of Islam are called Muslims. Their holy buildings are called mosques and their holy book is the Qur'an.

IRAN'S PEOPLES

STATISTICS

Today Iran's population includes several major **ethnic groups**.

Persian	51%
Azeri	24%
Gilaki and Mazandrani	8%
Kurd	7%
Arab	3%
Other	7%

The Persian Empire was swamped by the Islamic Arab Empire, which spread to include large parts of Africa, Asia, and Europe. The conquered lands became known as the "Islamic world."

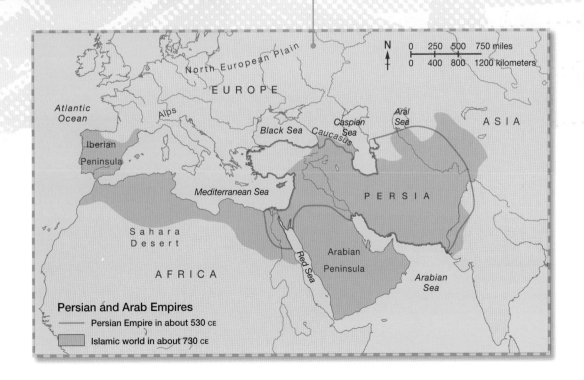

Persian and Arab Empires
— Persian Empire in about 530 CE
Islamic world in about 730 CE

PERSIA AND ISLAM

The conquered Persians converted to Islam. Over the next few hundred years, Persia became an important part of the new Islamic world. Persian scientists, artists, and writers were all involved in what became known as the Golden Age of Islamic culture.

Sunnis and Shi'as

In the early years of Islam, a major dispute broke out between Muslims. They could not agree over how their leader should be chosen. Two sides formed, called the Sunnis and the Shi'ites. They all remained Muslims, but over hundreds of years the differences between them grew. There were many more Sunnis in the Islamic world, but more Shi'ites than Sunnis in Persia.

HOT SPOT BRIEFING

WHO SHOULD LEAD?
After Mohammed's death, the Sunnis chose the prophet's advisor Abu Bakr to be the Muslim leader. The Shi'ites wanted Mohammed's cousin Ali to take the role. This dispute between electing a leader and following the family line remains important to the two groups today.

The Sheikh Lotfollah Mosque in the Persian city of Isfahan is an example of great Islamic building and artwork. It was built in 1615. The dome is covered in mosaic tiles.

The Long Decline

In the 1200s, Persia was invaded by the Mongols, nomadic warriors from Central Asia. More than half of the Persian population was killed. Many hundreds of years later, the country still had not fully recovered. In the 1800s, Western powers began getting involved in Persian affairs as a way of gaining influence in Asia. The Persians could do little to stop them.

In about 1255, Hulagu Khan, seen here with his wife, Dokuz Khatun, became the first Mongol ruler (or *Il-khan*) of Persia.

"The heart was carved out of Persia and its wealth, dragged off for Mongol use, made way for desolation. Half a dozen centuries would not bring back the prosperity and happiness that had existed before…"

British historian Peter Brent, in his book *The Mongol Empire* (1976).

OIL AND MODERNIZATION

The development of motor transport around 1900 made the world's rich countries hungry for oil. In 1908, British companies discovered major oilfields in southern Persia. The British government persuaded the Persians that British control of these oilfields was in everyone's interests.

The Majlis and Reza Khan

In 1907, a Persian parliament called the Majlis had been introduced. However, many of its members distrusted the British. In 1921, the British helped an army officer named Reza Khan seize power from the Majlis.

"It will provide all our ships east of Suez with fuel; it will strengthen British influence in these parts."

British officer Lieutenant Wilson describes the discovery of oil in Persia in 1908.

Workers for the Anglo-Iranian Oil Company gather in 1909 at a drilling tower, or derrick. The machinery drills for oil deep under the ground.

New Rule, New Name

In 1925, Reza Khan took the name Reza Shah (shah was the old Persian name for emperor). He began a program of **modernization**, which included more rights for women. He changed the country's name to Iran.

Reza's Son

In the late 1930s, Reza Shah grew close to Britain's enemy, Germany. In 1941, the British forced him to step down in favor of his son Muhammad. A new Majlis was elected. The British hoped that the new shah, Muhammad, would work together with the new Majlis to create a modern, pro-Western Iran.

HOT SPOT BRIEFING

REMOVING THE VEIL
Islamic tradition encourages modesty among women. This includes wearing loose clothing and, in strict cases, a veil over the face. As part of his modernization program, Reza Shah ordered his police to tear off women's veils.

In this photo from 1925, Reza Shah poses with a group of officers from the Persian army.

THE FIGHT FOR IRAN'S OIL

The British hoped that the Majlis would let them keep control of Iran's oil industry. However, the Majlis leader Mohammed Mossadeq was a **nationalist**. He put his own nation's interests first. He thought that Iran should control its own oil.

Mossadeq Takes Action

In 1951, Mossadeq successfully transferred the oil industry to Iranian ownership. This was not popular with the British, or their American **allies**. Over the next two years, the British and American **intelligence services** helped their supporters in Iran to plot against Mossadeq. In 1953, the Majlis leader was arrested and imprisoned for **treason**.

TOP FOUR FOR OIL

STATISTICS

In 1939, when World War II broke out, Iran was the world's fourth-largest oil producer. Only the United States, Russia, and Venezuela produced more.

Mohammed Mossadeq's challenge to the shah and his Western friends ended in failure. He spent the rest of his life in prison or confined to his home.

Muhammad Backs the West

The young Shah Muhammad backed the British–American plot. He left Iran for a while, fearing that he was in danger from the Majlis supporters. After Mossadeq's arrest, he returned to the capital, Tehran, in triumph. The Americans now considered the shah a valuable friend. Many Iranians, though, never forgave him for siding with foreigners against his own people.

HOT SPOT BRIEFING

NATIONALISTS
In the 1900s, people who fought for freedom from foreign control were called nationalists. Since these nations were usually poor, most nationalists emphasized the importance of **economic development**.

The Majlis meet in 1951, in their official chamber in Tehran. At this time, most Majlis members were against the shah.

THE SHAH'S IRAN

Once back in power, the shah tried to make sure he would stay there. He reduced the powers of the Majlis and expanded his armed forces. He also set up a much-feared **security police** force to keep an eye on his opponents.

The "White Revolution"

In 1963, the shah introduced a set of changes known as the "White Revolution." He aimed to make Iran stronger and richer. He wanted:

- a new organization to teach reading and writing in villages
- women to be given the vote
- land to be taken from the very rich and given to the poor
- to modernize the economy.

Much of Iran's income came from its oil sales. Big rises in oil prices in the 1970s meant that there was plenty of money for these new projects to go ahead.

In 1967, Shah Muhammad crowned himself and his queen, Queen Farah. He had delayed this ceremony because he did not want to wear the crown until he had made changes in his country.

America's Friend

When it came to dealing with the rest of the world, the shah relied on his friendship with the United States. He bought lots of American weapons. He also made secret military ties with America's other great friend in the region, Israel. Iran grew stronger. However, the close links with Israel and the United States upset other Islamic countries, such as Iraq and Syria.

HOT SPOT BRIEFING

AN EXPENSIVE PARTY
In October 1971, the shah held a large, very expensive celebration to mark 2,500 years of the Persian Empire. His extravagance angered many Iranians, who felt that he had more interest in himself than in his people.

The Shah makes a speech to visiting foreign rulers during the anniversary celebrations of October 1971.

"The Shi'ite clergy [religious officials] are the enemy of progress."
Shah Muhammad, speaking of the Islamic figures who opposed him in the 1970s.

THE ISLAMIC REVOLUTION

The shah's policies made Iran a more modern country. They also cost him the support of his people. By the end of the 1970s, the shah had made enemies throughout Iran. Revolution was stirring.

How the Shah Made Enemies

The shah was unpopular for various reasons.

1 His treatment of the Majlis angered Iranians who wanted more democracy, in other words, the chance to choose who governed their country.

2 His friendship with the United States, and the presence of many Americans in Tehran, upset nationalists.

3 His encouragement of Western lifestyles, particularly equality for women, angered the Islamic **clergy** and many other Muslims.

4 His economic changes produced more wealth for the country, but little of this went to the poor.

"American women clad in skimpy shorts and halters strode through the ancient Friday mosque, talking and laughing while Muslims prayed..."

American author Sandra Mackey gives an example of behavior during the shah's rule that offended Iranian citizens.

In January 1979, huge crowds of protesters gathered in Tehran to demonstrate against the shah and support a change in rule.

Ayatollah Khomeini

The most popular figure opposing the shah was the outspoken religious leader Ayatollah Khomeini. The ayatollah was in **exile**, having been sent away in 1964 by the shah. Through 1978, a campaign of demonstrations, strikes, and riots shook the cities of Iran. In January 1979, the shah was finally forced from power. Khomeini returned in triumph.

HOT SPOT BRIEFING

GETTING HIS MESSAGE ACROSS
While Ayatollah Khomeini was in exile, his followers recorded his speeches on tape. Copies were made, and thousands of cassettes were then smuggled into Iran.

Ayatollah Khomeini (left) is greeted by supporters in February 1979, on his return to Iran. Khomeini had spent the last fifteen years in exile in Iraq and France.

A NEW DISPUTE

On April 1, 1979, Iran became an **Islamic republic** with Khomeini in charge. Since the revolution, though, a new dispute had emerged. While almost all Iranians had wanted to end the shah's rule, they were divided over what came next.

United Against America

The only area of agreement among Iranians was **foreign policy**. Most of the population wanted to end Iran's friendship with the United States. In November 1979, a mob seized the U.S. Embassy in Tehran and took the staff **hostage**. Iranians countrywide supported the capture.

Anti-American crowds gather in November 1979, in support of the hostage-takers at Tehran's U.S. Embassy. The hostages were eventually released after 444 days in captivity.

Divided Over Rule

There were two very different views on how Iran should be governed. The traditionalist clergy and their supporters wanted to run the country as a religious state, with strict Islamic laws and rules. The nationalists wanted a modernized Iran, run by an elected Majlis.

The Traditionalists' Victory

For several years, the nationalists and traditionalists fought it out. What started as arguments soon turned to violence, with regular bombings and executions. By 1982, several thousand people had been killed. The traditionalists were victorious.

HOT SPOT BRIEFING

THE REVOLUTIONARY GUARDS
In 1979, a new military force was created alongside the regular Iranian army. Its role was to defend the clergy and their supporters against enemies both within and outside Iran. Its soldiers became known as the Revolutionary Guards.

The Revolutionary Guards included women as well as men. Part of their role was to help enforce the rules laid down by the Islamic leaders.

THE ISLAMIC REPUBLIC

In the new Islamic Republic, Islam was central to everyday life. All Iranian rules and laws, and every person's behavior, would have to be acceptable to the religious leadership.

Division of Power

Power in the Islamic Republic was divided four ways, between:

- the Majlis
- the president
- the Council of Guardians
- the supreme religious leader, or Faqih.

The elected Majlis and president could propose new policies and laws. These could be overruled by the Council of Guardians, which was made up of leading religious officials. The Faqih made all final decisions. The Ayatollah Khomeini was the Faqih until his death in 1989.

"This is not an ordinary government. It is a government based on Islamic law."

Ayatollah Khomeini, speaking at a press conference in February 1979.

In 1982, Ali Khamene'i, a former leader of the Revolutionary Guards, became president. He later went on to become supreme leader.

Pleasing Some, Disappointing Others

For many Iranians, the republic was proving a success. Their traditional culture was well protected, and the country's foreign policy favored the Islamic world. Others were disappointed. Iran was no more democratic than it had been before. Iranians could vote, but only for certain parties or people. Men had no more freedom, and women had less.

A group of Iranian schoolchildren study prayer in 1982. The girls are wearing traditional Islamic dress. Women who tried to wear modern clothes were often arrested or beaten. Today, girls are usually taught separately from boys.

THE WAR WITH IRAQ

In September 1980, Iran's neighbor, Iraq, began a war against Iran. Iraq's leader, Saddam Hussein, was afraid that the Iranian revolution would stir up trouble among Iraq's Shi'ite **minority**. He also hoped to conquer Iran's rich southern oilfields.

Support for Iraq

Other Middle Eastern leaders feared that the people in their countries might follow the Iranians' example and rise up in revolution, too. They gave money to help Saddam Hussein's Iraq. The Western powers agreed that Iran was a troublemaker and offered Hussein military help. The United States had not forgiven the Iranians for overthrowing their friend the shah, or for the embassy hostage-takings.

Iranian troops pray as they prepare to fight with Iraq in March 1985. Hundreds of thousands of soldiers died in the war against Iraq.

United in Suffering

The Iran–Iraq war lasted for nearly eight years. In Iran, most families suffered at least one death or injury. The economy, and particularly the oil industry, was badly hit. In some ways, the Islamic Republic was strengthened by the war with Iraq. Forced to defend themselves, the Iranian people stood loyally behind their government.

A LONG AND BLOODY WAR

STATISTICS

During the seven years and eleven months of war, more than one million people were killed. Around two-thirds of these were Iranian.

An Iranian boy stands on the ruins of his house in the city of Ahwaz. It was destroyed in January 1987 by an Iraqi air raid.

HARDLINERS AND MODERATES

Ayatollah Khomeini died in 1989. More than 12 million people lined the streets to see his funeral procession. The ayatollah had been a popular and powerful leader. There was no single strong leader to follow him. Arguments between Iranians became common.

Two Points of View

There were two main views on how the Islamic Republic should be governed after Khomeini's death. Two sides formed, the hardliners and the moderates.

1 The hardliners wanted to stick to a strict policy and insisted that Islamic rules should decide everything. If these got in the way of economic growth or winning friends abroad, then Iran would have to survive without the growth or the friends.

2 The moderates agreed that Islamic rules were important, but also pointed out how old they were. If Iran was to move forward, then there had to be compromises between these strict, ancient rules and a modern society.

"Today, the old civilization cannot be preserved. There must be change for modern times, appropriate to the circumstances."

The moderate President Khatami, speaking in 1997.

On 5 June 1989, the day before the ayatollah's funeral, his body was displayed in Tehran. Iranians flocked to pay their last respects to the leader, who died at age eighty-six.

Supreme Leaders and Presidents

Since Ayatollah Khomeini's death:

- Ayatollah Ali Khamene'i has been the supreme leader
- Akbar Rafsanjani, a moderate, was elected president in 1989
- another moderate, Mohammad Khatami, replaced him in 1997
- Mahmoud Ahmadinejad, a hardliner, replaced Khatami in 2005.

President Rafsanjani speaks at a rally in February 1993, held to celebrate the fourteenth anniversary of the Islamic Revolution.

TERRORISM AND THE NUCLEAR ISSUE

In recent years, Iran has faced fierce criticism from other countries. The claims the critics have made are:

- that Iranian governments are supporting **terrorism**
- that they are trying to acquire **nuclear weapons**.

Terrorists or Not?

The United States and the **European Union** accused Iran of giving money and military help to two groups that they consider to be terrorist. These are the Hezbollah in Lebanon and Hamas in Palestine. The Iranians admitted to supporting these groups, but denied that they were terrorist.

HOT SPOT BRIEFING

AXIS OF EVIL
In January 2002, President George W. Bush accused three countries of supporting terrorism and forming an "Axis of Evil."
They were:
- North Korea
- Iraq
- Iran.

This is the Bushehr nuclear power plant, which is located 746 miles (1,200 kilometers) south of Tehran. It is Iran's first nuclear power station and is being built with Russian help.

Weapons or Energy?

In 2002, the United States claimed that Iran was building nuclear weapons. Iran said that it was only developing peaceful **nuclear energy**. In November 2007, a report issued by an American intelligence agency supported the Iranian claim. Nonetheless, the United States refuses to rule out using military force to destroy Iran's nuclear sites.

Iranians Unite

Iranians seem united behind their government on these issues. Both hardliners and moderates are proud of their country's nuclear program. Both groups resent foreigners telling them what they can and cannot do.

"It is our judgment that Iran is developing a nuclear weapon."
U.S. Secretary of State Colin Powell in 2004.

"As we have often said, we are not making nuclear weapons."
Supreme Leader Ayatollah Khamene'i in 2004.

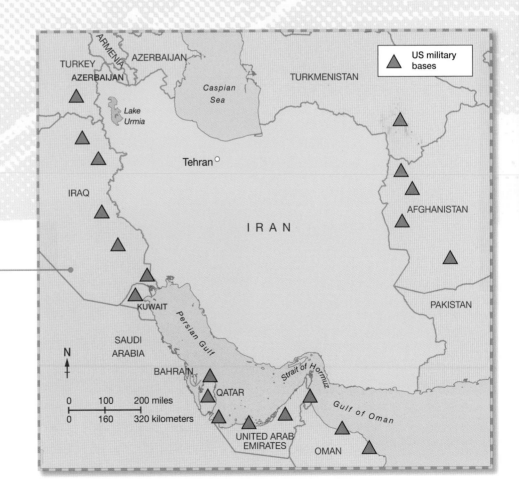

The United States has military bases in most of Iran's surrounding countries—Iraq, Afghanistan, Pakistan, Saudi Arabia, Bahrain, the United Arab Emirates, and Oman.

US military bases

TURKEY
ARMENIA
AZERBAIJAN
AZERBAIJAN
Caspian Sea
TURKMENISTAN
Lake Urmia
Tehran
IRAQ
IRAN
AFGHANISTAN
KUWAIT
Persian Gulf
SAUDI ARABIA
PAKISTAN
N
BAHRAIN
Strait of Hormuz
QATAR
Gulf of Oman
0   100   200 miles
0   160   320 kilometers
UNITED ARAB EMIRATES
OMAN

THE FUTURE FOR IRAN

Iran's future seems uncertain. There may be conflict with other countries over the nuclear program. Within Iran, there is growing tension between the religious government and modern society. Many people see a need for change.

Political Unrest

The Islamic Republic faces political difficulties. Politicians are less trusted than they used to be, mostly because so many have used their power to get rich. In addition, TV and the Internet have made ideas from outside Iran more popular. Women in particular know that their government deprives them of freedoms that women elsewhere take for granted.

HOT SPOT BRIEFING

WOMEN IN IRAN
Iranian women are kept apart from men in most public places, including schools. They are expected to wear clothes that cover all but their hands and faces. However, Iran has more women in higher education than most Muslim countries. The number of women in work has doubled since 1979.

President Mahmoud Ahmadinejad speaks in 2006 at a news conference in Tehran. When he was elected in 2005, he promised greater honesty from Iranian government officials.

Economic Outlook

There are also economic worries in Iran. The government has refused to let people make their own economic decisions. This has made it difficult for businesses to work efficiently, slowing economic growth for the country as a whole.

Caution Before Change

Despite these problems, Iran remains comfortable in many ways. Its enormous oil wealth still supports the economy. Many Iranians continue to back the government. A modern way of life might appeal to some, but others prefer the old ways. If changes are to come, they will probably come slowly.

LOTS OF OIL

STATISTICS

Iran's oil reserves are the third-largest in the world, after Saudi Arabia and Canada. They amount to around 133 billion barrels, or 88 years' production at the current rate.

Iranians surf the Internet at a cyber café in Tehran. Many Iranians rely on the Internet for unbiased news about their own country and the rest of the world.

FACTFINDER

GEOGRAPHY

Capital Tehran

Area 636,300 square miles
(1,648,000 square kilometers)

Main rivers Karun and Karkheh

Climate Mostly arid or semi-arid. Sub-tropical along the Caspian Sea coast

Land use   Farmland 11%

Other 89%

PEOPLE

Population 65,398,000 (2007 estimate)

Rate of population change +0.66 % per year

Life expectancy 70.6 years

Average age 25.8 years

Religions   Muslim 98%

(Shi'ite 89%, Sunni 9%)

Other 2%

Ethnic groups   Persian 51%

Azeri 24%

Gilaki and Mazandrani 8%

Kurd 7%

Arab 3%

Other 7%

Literacy   Men 84%

Women 70%

* Gross Domestic Product per person is the total value of all the goods and services produced by a country in a year divided by the number of people in the country.
(Source for statistics: *CIA World Factbook*, 2008)

THE ECONOMY

Agricultural products Wheat, rice, other grains, sugar crops, fruits, nuts, cotton, dairy products

Industries Petroleum, chemicals, fertilizers, textiles, construction materials, food processing

Main exports Petroleum, chemicals and petrochemicals, fruits and nuts, carpets

Gross Domestic Product per person*
$12,300

National earning by sector   Agriculture 11%

Industry 45%

Services 44%

HOT SPOT BRIEFING

A YOUNG NATION
Over 70 percent of Iran's population has been born since the revolution in 1979.

The flag of Iran

GLOSSARY

allies supporters

Arabian peninsula large, mostly desert area bordered by the Red Sea, Arabian Sea, and Persian Gulf

clergy religious officials

culture things that make a group of people distinctive, such as their language, clothes, food, music, songs and stories

economic development expanding and improving industry, agriculture, and transportation facilities

empire large group of countries ruled by a single country

European Union political and economic organization that links and speaks for most of Europe's independent countries

exile forced absence from one's own country

foreign policy dealing with other countries

hostage prisoner, held in order to gain political advantage

intelligence services government agencies that gather secret information about other countries

Islamic based on Islam, one of the world's major religions, founded by the Prophet Mohammed in the 600s

Islamic republic region governed according to the laws of Islam

minority smallest group

modernization starting to use the latest ideas, techniques, and equipment

nationalist someone who puts his or her own nation above all others

nomads herders who move from place to place to find food for their animals

nuclear energy energy produced by splitting or combining atoms

nuclear weapons powerful bombs or missiles that use nuclear energy

secular nonreligious

security police police who protect the government from its enemies

terrorism the use of violence to scare people

traditionalists (in the Middle East) people who believe that Westernization and modernization threaten traditional Islamic culture

treason acting against one's own country

Western characteristic of North America and Western Europe, and their systems of electing governments

INDEX